Why Do We Wear Ashes?
Nine Lenten Chancel Dramas
By Paul L. Larsen

C.S.S. Publishing Co.
Lima, Ohio

WHY DO WE WEAR ASHES?
NINE LENTEN CHANCEL DRAMAS

Copyright © 1991 by
The C.S.S. Publishing Company, Inc.
Lima, Ohio

All rights reserved. No part of this publication may be reproduced, stored in a retrieval system, or transmitted in any form or by any means, electronic, mechanical, photocopying, recording, or otherwise, without the prior permission of the publisher. Inquiries should be addressed to: The C.S.S. Publishing Company, Inc., 628 South Main Street, Lima, Ohio 45804.

Library of Congress Cataloging-in-Publication Data

Larsen, Paul, 1947-
    Why do we wear ashes? : nine Lenten chancel dramas / by Paul Larsen.
       p.   cm.
    ISBN 1-55673-284-8
    1. Lent — Drama. 2. Drama in public worship. 3. Christian drama. American. I. Title.
PS3562.A744W48   1991
246'.7—dc20   90-47104
                                                                                           CIP

9117 / ISBN 1-55673-284-8   PRINTED IN U.S.A.

Dedicated to:
The members of Hope Lutheran Church, Jordan Minnesota, who encouraged the writing, performance and eventual publication of these dramas.

TABLE OF CONTENTS

Introduction 7

Why Do We Wear Ashes? 9
    A drama for Ash Wednesday

Why Do We Sing Hymns? 15

Why Do We Confess Our Sins? 21

Why Do We Give? 27

Why Do We Baptize? 35

Why Do We Commune? 43
    A drama for Lutheran Churches —
    Setting is an early communion instruction class

Why Do We Commune? 51
    A drama for non-Lutheran congregations

Why Do We Confirm Our Faith? 57

Why Do We Worship So Often? 65
    A drama for Maundy Thursday

INTRODUCTION

Chancel dramas are not unique. They have been used to involve laity in leading Lenten worship for years. These dramas, however, have some unique features. They incorporate youth and children in the cast. Many young people are anxious for some meaningful involvement as worship leaders, and they can find some fulfillment in playing these roles. Having youthful cast members also makes watching these dramas more interesting for the young people attending worship. Another unique feature is the subject matter. The rites and rituals of the church can become so routine for church members that they forget the reasoning behind them. Both children and adults may wonder "Why do we wear ashes on Ash Wednesday?"; "Why do we worship so often during Holy Week?"; "Why do we affirm our baptismal vows?" These dramas seek to offer some answers in a concise, interesting, and sometimes humorous way.

The dramas are meant to reflect real life and are written the way people usually speak. Contractions abound, especially when the youth are speaking: "What do you" is contracted to "Wha'da'ya';" "Going to" is contracted to "gonna;" "Don't you" becomes "Doncha," etc.

It is not necessary for the cast to memorize their lines. Reader's theater can be very effective, and people are much more willing to be involved if they can use a script.

The author of these dramas had two goals in mind: first, to help people grow in their understanding of the faith and the rites and rituals of the church; and, second, to enable both youth and adults to find some joy and fulfillment as worship leaders. Hopefully, those goals will be met as you use these dramas in your congregation.

Congregations are encouraged to develop these dramas in settings specific to their own situation. You may wish, for example, to substitute names or descriptions of certain characters. You may wish to modify the dialogue to fit your own locale. You may consider giving some of the dramas at a time of the year other than Lent. For example, "Why Do We Give," could be used effectively during a period of stewardship.

Each drama is approximately 10 minutes in length.

WHY DO WE WEAR ASHES?

A drama for Ash Wednesday

Cast of Characters:

    JIM WASHINGTON: A jovial older gentleman, late 50s, early 60s.
    ANN CHRISTIANSON: Young, articulate mother of two — ashes on her forehead.
    BEN CHRISTIANSON: Nine to eleven-year-old boy — ashes on his forehead.
    BETH CHRISTIANSON: Six-year-old girl — ashes on her forehead.
    FRED KREUSER: Serious, questioning man in his late 40s, early 50s.

Setting:

The local grocery store. Ann, Ben, and Beth should have a grocery cart with a few items in it. They should have crosses of ashes on their foreheads. *(They have just come from Ash Wednesday worship.)* **Jim and Fred can be carrying grocery baskets.**

JIM: Hi, there, Ann. Hey, kids. Fancy meeting you in the grocery store. I guess the Christianson family eats, too!

ANN: That's an understatement! Especially Ben here — he can eat more than I can for dinner and then want something an hour later. I sometimes wonder if he doesn't have a hollow leg!

JIM: Say, what have you been into? You have dirt on your forehead.

ANN: Dirt? *(Taking out her compact and looking in the mirror)* Oh, that. I forgot all about it — we just came from Ash Wednesday worship service.

JIM: You all have it on you. I didn't know your church was so dirty! I know the name of a good janitorial service.

ANN: Jim, this isn't dirt — it is ashes.

JIM: What? Do you burn wood up there now, or what?

ANN: No, it's part of the service.

BEN: The pastor puts ashes on our forehead.

JIM: And you let him do that? Sounds pretty strange to me. What is it, some kind of seal of approval? Or a stamp that lets you leave and come back in later, like at a dance?

(Enter Fred)

JIM: Hey, Fred, come here! Look at Ann and the kids here. They go to church and come out all dirty. I thought going to church was supposed to cleanse you of your sins! *(Laughs)*

FRED: I didn't know your church was into ashes and such. What's it supposed to mean anyway?

ANN: Well, it's a symbol . . .

BETH: When the pastor puts it on me, he said I was dust.

FRED: He said you were dust! That sounds uplifting and inspiring!

ANN: Give me a minute and I'll explain. You see, Ash Wednesday is the beginning of Lent.

BEN: That's a season of 40 days. A season of repentance.

ANN: That's right, Ben. Ashes have always been a symbol of repentance or turning back from our sins and trying to live in a new way. They are a symbol of death and renewal. Like when the farmers used to burn their fields in the spring to destroy the old and prepare for the new.

JIM: So, why do you tell these poor kids they are dirt — that doesn't make them feel very good about themselves.

BETH: I'm not dirt. I'm dust and to dust I shall return. So are you — so is everybody.

ANN: That's right, Beth, we are all dust and these ashes remind us that some day we will die.

FRED: Do you think it is good to be scaring kids, talking about death and being dust? They haven't even started to live yet! It doesn't sound like a very healthy attitude to me. I mean, I don't go to church, but I watch it on television and those television preachers are always saying, "You can do anything," "Think positively!" "If life gives you a lemon, make lemonade!" That sounds a lot better for kids to hear than this depressing dust and ashes stuff.

ANN: Well, there's more to it than that. It isn't just dust and ashes, it is also a sign of the cross. The cross reminds us that Jesus died for us. While we are merely dust and we are destined to die because of our sin, Jesus died for us. His death and his resurrection promise us new life.

FRED: That sounds a little more optimistic. But, why all the repentance, dust and death talk to go along with it?

ANN: Like it or not, we're all going to die. It doesn't do us any good to deny that. In fact, if we can face our mortality and face the fact that we're going to die, it can help us get more out of life.

JIM: How so?

ANN: Well, it reminds us to live life to the fullest. To use the gift of life God has given us. It tells us to do what we can for God and for His people right now!

JIM: I'm not sure I understand.

ANN: If you think you are going to live forever, you can easily waste your time. But, if you know there is a limit, you use it more wisely.

BEN: You mean like when we take a test in school. Everyone really starts to work when the teacher says there's only five minutes left.

ANN: Right. Or when we are getting ready for company. The closer it is to their arrival time, the faster and harder we work.

BETH: Or like getting ready for school. I usually get more done in the last 10 minutes before the bus comes than I did the whole rest of the hour I've been up.

ANN: You sure do, sweetheart. We work differently under deadlines. Being reminded of our mortality also reminds us to get busy and live life now. I think it can be a positive thing rather than negative.

FRED: Well, I for one would rather listen to a television preacher tell me things I want to hear.

ANN: Maybe that's easier to hear, but just make sure it's the truth you are hearing. It's hard to make lemonade when the lemon you are handed is death. But because of the cross, something that sounds like negative news, God gives us the gift of forgiveness and new life. I feel it's important to acknowledge the fact that I haven't earned that with my own good works and to recognize my need to repent. Then I can better appreciate the real gift God has given me.

BEN: No matter what we think, Mr. Kreuser, we're dust, and to dust we shall return.

ANN: The good news is, God can raise us up from that condition and give us new life.

JIM: Well, I'd better finish getting my groceries, or my wife will turn me into dust before my time!

FRED: Me, too! It's been an interesting conversation, though. You've given me some things to think about.

ANN: If you want to talk about it more sometime, I would be happy to. You are both welcome to come and worship with us at our church any time.

FRED AND JIM: Thanks. See you later.

BETH: Mom, can we go wash these ashes off? Otherwise, we are going to spend the whole night here talking about Ash Wednesday.

ANN: These ashes sure do get people talking, don't they? Maybe we should wear something like this more often. It certainly seems to open the door for conversation about God. Let's see if we can't find the rest of our groceries.

— The End —

WHY DO WE SING HYMNS?

Cast of Characters:

    JIM CLASSIC: Sixteen-year-old rock music fan.
    MR. EARL CLASSIC: Jim's father. Mid-forties. Rather opinionated.
    MRS. ELAINE CLASSIC: Jim's mother. Mid-forties. A peacemaker. Quite open-minded.
    CAROL CLASSIC: Jim's 14-year-old sister.

Setting:

In the Classic's living room. Mr. Classic is sitting in a chair, reading the paper, when Jim comes into the room with the boom box blasting. Mrs. Classic and daughter, Carol, enter room together some time later.

(Jim enters the room with boom box on his shoulder, blaring his favorite hit song. He is really into the music and he is moving with it.)

MR. CLASSIC: Jim, turn that terrible thing down!

JIM: Hey, Dad, this's my favorite song — don'tcha like it? It's really got a beat!

MR. CLASSIC: I know, and it's beating my brains out. Please turn that junk down!

JIM: *(Turns music off)* You call my music junk? At least it's better'n that garbage you like. That classical stuff you listen to bores me to death.

MR. CLASSIC: Hey, that's great music. You should learn to appreciate it.

JIM: That's probably all they had back in prehistoric times when you were growing up — just kidding, just kidding. You didn't really listen to that when you were my age, didja?

MR. CLASSIC: Well, no, I developed a taste for classical music when I matured. When I was growing up, we had much better music than you kids have today. I mean, you could understand the words and actually sing along. Your music's mostly noise.

JIM: I've heard some'a the old stuff you liked so much. It really had wonderful words. I mean like "She bop, she bop" really means a lot to me.

MR. CLASSIC: That does sound a little silly, but some of the songs really had a message.

JIM: Well, some'a today's songs really have a message, too.

MRS. CLASSIC: *(enters room with Carol, her daughter)* What're you two arguing about?

MR. CLASSIC: We aren't arguing. We're discussing music. I'm explaining how much better our music was and is than the junk Jim listens to.

JIM: And I'm explaining how much better modern stuff is than your moldy oldies.

MRS. CLASSIC: Well, it seems to me you both ought to stop arguing and accept the fact that different music speaks to different people.

CAROL: The church ought'a recognize that, too.

MRS. CLASSIC: Wha'da'ya mean?

CAROL: I mean they ought'a offer more variety. Seems like we sing all the same old boring hymns all the time. Most of 'em were written hundreds'a years ago and they don't say anything to me.

MR. CLASSIC: Now, I'm not sure that's completely true. I noticed you wipe a tear away during "Silent Night" at the Christmas Eve Candlelight Service.

CAROL: That's different. That's a Christmas carol and it was a really meaningful service.

MRS. CLASSIC: Well, I've seen you sing some other hymns you seem to enjoy.

CAROL: Some of 'em are okay, but I like the songs we sing at camp a lot better. They're faster paced and more fun to sing.

JIM: Can'tcha just see Elmer Stucker singin' camp songs in church! Now, there's someone who's hooked on the classics. He thinks everything's gotta be 500 years old before you sing it or listen to it.

MR. CLASSIC: I don't think he would mind so much. I mean he really does appreciate music. I think he recognizes how important music is to the worship service.

JIM: If it's so important, then we should have some better music!

MR. CLASSIC: I don't know how you can judge that. You never open your hymnal or your mouth during the service.

MRS. CLASSIC: Now, Earl, just be glad Jim's there. Although I do agree, Jim, that you'd enjoy the service more and get more out of it if you joined in the singing. I know you can sing — you sing along with your boom box lots of times.

JIM: That's different. I like this music.

MR. CLASSIC: But some of the hymns we sing really carry a great message. Don't tell me you can't feel the power of some of the great Easter hymns we sing.

JIM: Well, I'll admit that some of 'em are okay. In fact, sometimes they say more to me than the sermon does. But most'a the time we sing some real losers.

MRS. CLASSIC: I have to admit that there are some hymns in the hymnal that aren't very singable, but there are some really good ones, too. Hymns are poetry set to music and, as such, they offer us a unique way to express our faith. Music and poetry can speak more eloquently than just words can. They can express our frailty and tragedy and the wonder of God's grace in a very meaningful way.

CAROL: Yeah, I like the hymn, "Amazing Grace." I think we should sing that one more often.

JIM: I suppose if ya think about it, there are **some** good hymns. I just think we should sing more hymns that're fun to sing.

MRS. CLASSIC: You know, the kids may have something here. Maybe the church should use some more contemporary music. I mean, the point of hymn singing is to help people offer their praise to God. If young people could relate to more modern music, maybe the church should use some more contemporary songs. After all, kids are a part of the church, too.

MR. CLASSIC: I've got a good idea, Jim. Why don't you talk to Pastor White about your ideas about more contemporary hymns? Maybe you could even be on the worship committee and help pick out the hymns.

JIM: Naw, he'd never listen to me. I'm just'a dumb kid as far as he's concerned.

MR. CLASSIC: That's not true. I may think of you that way — just kidding. I had to get you back for that "prehistoric" comment. I'm sure he'd be interested in your ideas, and if you asked to serve on the worship committee, he'd be overjoyed. People hardly ever volunteer for anything. Give it a try — you don't have anything to lose.

JIM: Maybe I will. If hymns are 'spose'ta be something that helps us offer our praise to God, then I think we should sing some that everyone can relate to, not just adults. It's been nice talkin' to you dudes, but I hafta go do my homework now. *(Turns radio back on real loud and dances his way off stage.)*

— The End —

WHY DO WE CONFESS OUR SINS?

Cast of Characters:

    MS. LUANA BLACK: A Sunday school teacher, open-minded, likes to let the kids talk and share ideas.
    LISA LEMON: An inquisitive Sunday school student.
    DAVID FONG: An intelligent youth who has some good insights.
    ROSA CAMPOS: A bright young student who contributes to the discussion and asks good questions.
    PHILIP STONE: A mature student who is willing to share some of his own experiences.

Setting:

A Sunday school classroom.

MS. BLACK: Good morning, class.

ALL: Good morning, Ms. Black.

MS. BLACK: Let's begin our session with prayer.

(All bow heads and fold hands.)

O Lord, be with us as we begin our study of worship. Help us to learn more about why we do what we do in worship. Let us learn and grow so that our worship service is more meaningful to us.
Amen.

Now, how many of you were at the first service this morning? *(Some students raise hands)* Good. Was there anything that happened today that you have questions about?

(Lisa raises hand)

Lisa.

LISA: I have a question, but it isn't about this morning necessarily. I mean, we do this almost every Sunday and I wonder why. Why do we always hafta confess our sins? I don't like being reminded of my sins.

MS. BLACK: Well, why do you think we do?

LISA: I dunno. That's why I'm asking.

DAVID: *(raising hand)* I think I know. We use a confession of sins because we're sinners and we need to hear an announcement of forgiveness.

LISA: Yeah, but God already knows about all our sins. He knows more about them than we do — so why go through that all the time?

ROSA: I think we hafta confess our sins so God can forgive us.

MS. BLACK: That's certainly part of the reason we confess our sins. But, do you think we **have** to confess our sins so God can forgive us? Sometimes we may not even know that something we did was wrong. Do you think God will refuse to forgive us just because we didn't mention a particular sin in our confession?

DAVID: I don't think so. I mean, if we don't know what we did was wrong or if we forget to confess something, God'll still forgive us. He forgives our sins because he loves us, not because we remembered to confess them.

LISA: That's what I mean. Why do we bother with it? God'll forgive us anyway.

PHILIP: I think we confess our sins because, as they say, "It is good for the soul."

LISA: Wha'da'ya mean?

PHILIP: If we've done something wrong and don't admit it, we end up feeling guilty about it. I remember when I was about six my sister and I were staying with my grandparents. My grandpa made me a sling shot. I was terrible with it. I couldn't even hit the side of the barn. I was goofing around with it and I saw my grandmother's pet duck. I put a pebble in the sling, flipped it at the duck and hit poor old "Quacker" right on the head and killed him dead.

LISA: "Quacker!" — what a stupid name!

PHILIP: Your name isn't anything to brag about either, Lemon.

DAVID: So what happened?

PHILIP: I pretended like nothing happened. Nobody said anything about it at supper so I figured nobody saw me. Then my sister whispered in my ear, "Either you do the dishes for me tonight or I'll tell Grandma that you killed Quacker." She blackmailed me for two days. But that wasn't the worst of it. I felt so guilty about it I finally told my grandmother what had happened. She said she had seen me do it too, and wondered how long it would take for me to admit it and how long I was going to put up with my sister's blackmail.

ROSA: Did she punish you?

PHILIP: No, she said she forgave me and she felt I'd been punished enough already over the last two days. But, she did say she hoped I'd learned something.

ROSA: So, what didja learn?

PHILIP: To never shoot my sling shot at something I didn't want to hit and to get good enough with it to shoot at my sister!

(Students all laugh)

MS. BLACK: Philip, that's a terrible thing to say!

PHILIP: No, what I really learned is that when you do something wrong it's better to admit it than try to hide it. Confession may not be easy, but it makes you feel better when it's over.

DAVID: You're right. I remember one time I accidentally broke a vase in the house. I was throwin' a pillow at my bratty little brother. I missed and this expensive vase crashed into a thousand pieces. I knew I had ta tell my mom before my brother did, but I sure didn't like it. I didn't enjoy being grounded over it either, but even that wasn't as bad as the guilt and fear I felt before I told Mom what happened.

ROSA: It sounds like your mom didn't forgive you.

DAVID: Why?

ROSA: Well, you got grounded.

DAVID: I don't think that means she didn't forgive me. My brother and I had been warned about "pillow fights" before and I knew what would happen — I just didn't think I'd miss. No, my mom forgave me. She told me she loved me and that she wanted me ta learn something from this. She also said I knew beforehand that if I got in a pillow fight again, I'd get grounded, so I had made my choice.

ROSA: It seems like parents always want'cha ta learn something from stuff.

MS. BLACK: I think God wants us to learn, too. In his love and forgiveness, he wants us to learn how to be better people. When we confess our sins and admit them to God, we're recognizing that we need to make a change in our life. When he forgives us, he gives us the strength and desire to change.

PHILIP: I guess when I think about it, the confession of sins and the announcement of forgiveness is one of the most important parts of the service for me. Even if Pastor Long's sermon is boring, I can at least have heard that my sins are forgiven.

MS. BLACK: It seems we have come up with some good answers for your question, Lisa. We use a confession of sins because (1) God asks us to confess our sins and promises to forgive us; (2) because we feel better when we admit what we have done wrong; and (3) because we need to hear the message that God forgives us. What do you think?

LISA: I 'spose those are good answers. It's just that sometimes Pastor Long lives up to his name and I was looking for a way to shorten things up a little.

PHILIP: Well, maybe if **you** didn't have so many sins to confess, that part of the service wouldn't take so long!

ALL: *(Laugh)*

MS. BLACK: Class, we're out of time, but I want to thank you for a good discussion today. While we didn't get into our lesson exactly, we did discuss something important about worship. Let's close with a prayer.

(All fold hands and bow heads)

O God, we give you thanks that we know we can confess our sins and that you will forgive us. Help us to remember that no sin is too big for you to forgive. Let your word of forgiveness strengthen us and enable us to live like forgiven and loved people. Amen.

— The End —

WHY DO WE GIVE?

Cast of Characters:

    DAN BEAN: Inquisitive, outgoing high school student.
    MR. GREG BEAN: Dan's father, an accountant. Somewhat defensive with Dan, but rather aggressive with Pastor Givens.
    PASTOR GIVENS: Pastor of Community of Hope Church. Late 30s-early 40s.

Setting:

Scene I. Mr. Bean's office at home. He has a stack of bills in front of him, as well as the check book and a calculator. One of the envelopes on his desk is the church offering envelope. Dan comes home from school and finds Mr. Bean paying the household bills.

Scene II. Pastor Given's office. Setting can be a desk and a couple of chairs or you could set up a love seat arrangement if time and space permit. Just make sure the set can be changed quickly and efficiently.

DAN: Hi, Dad, what're you doin'?

MR. BEAN: *(sarcastically)* My favorite job — paying the bills.

DAN: Hey, that's great! This works perfectly. I was gonna ask ya about what things cost for a project we're doin' in school. Do we have a household budget I could see? We're 'spos'ta figure out what it costs to operate an average household per month.

MR. BEAN: Now, wait a minute. Who's gonna see these figures? I don't care to have the whole school know about our income and expenses.

DAN: Take it easy, Dad. No one's gonna know whose numbers are whose. Mr. Rodriguez, our social studies teacher, was very specific about how each of us would enter our figures into the computer anonymously. He said we'd do it that way because most people're more secretive about finances than they are about sex! *(laughs)*

MR. BEAN: *(defensively)* Well, I just don't happen to think this is anybody's business. I'm not even sure you need to know — you'll probably blab about it to your friends.

DAN: Hey, I promise. I just wanna learn somethin' here. You're always sayin' I don't know the value of a dollar. How can you expect me ta learn how much everything costs if you keep it all a secret?

MR. BEAN: All right. But just remember this isn't public information. Wha'da'ya want to know?

DAN: Let's just start with the bills you've got there in front of ya. What's that first one — the electric bill? *(Dan takes out a pad and pencil to record the numbers.)*

MR. BEAN: Yes. It cost $65 this month.

DAN: Whoa, that's high!

MR. BEAN: It wouldn't be that high if you'd ever remember to turn off some lights or the television or didn't stand there staring into the fridge with the door open for hours on end!

DAN: Easy! Easy! I'll watch it. See, I'm learnin' somethin' from this already! What's next?

MR. BEAN: The heat bill. It runs $150 a month in the winter.

DAN: It's a good thing it hasn't been very cold this month. How about the mortgage payment — what's that?

MR. BEAN: Six hundred and fifty dollars a month.

DAN: That's less than I thought. Jeff Little said their new house was gonna run over $1,000 a month.

MR. BEAN: Well, this house is 12 years old and we have a lower interest rate.

DAN: What else have ya got?

MR. BEAN: The phone bill runs $30 a month — that is, if your mother doesn't get lonesome for her family in Florida — then it jumps to $50 a month. Car insurance runs $80 a month. Gas and maintenance for the cars — about $100 a month. Life insurance $100 a month . . .

DAN: What's that one there?

MR. BEAN: Oh, that's our offering for the church.

DAN: Do you consider that a bill?

MR. BEAN: I pay it like a bill. Otherwise, I'm afraid I'll fall behind.

DAN: Forty dollars a month, huh? Gee, that's about the smallest bill we've got! Is that what you call a ti thee? *(TI THEE)*

MR. BEAN: What's a Ti Thee? *(TI THEE)*

DAN: I dunno. We studied about it in our high school class at church last week. The lesson was somethin' about ti thees and offerings.

MR. BEAN: Oh, you mean tithe *(T-I-T-H-E)*. No, a tithe is giving ten percent of your income.

DAN: How come we don't do that? The teacher said that's what the Bible recommends.

MR. BEAN: *(obviously a little flustered)* Well, ah, I dunno. That's just a suggestion from the Old Testament. We live by grace and we're able to give whatever we feel like.

DAN: Oh, I guess I was just surprised it was one of the smallest amounts we pay for anything. Are there any other regular bills I should know about?

MR. BEAN: Wha'da'ya think? Have we plugged anything in for food, or clothing, or entertainment yet? You do need to learn some things about what it costs to run a household, don't you . . . ?

Have someone walk across in front with signs saying, "END OF SCENE ONE. APPLAUD."
Announce "We Give Thee But Thine Own" or another appropriate stewardship hymn to be sung during set change.

Set Up For Scene Two

Mr. Bean knocks on the pastor's office door.

PASTOR GIVENS: Come on in. Oh, hi, Greg. How are you?

MR. BEAN: Fine. Just fine. Have you gotta minute to talk?

PASTOR GIVENS: Sure. Have a seat. What can I do for you?

MR. BEAN: You can tell me how much I should give to the church.

PASTOR GIVENS: Tell you how much to give to the church! I don't know how I can do that, Greg. I mean, that's something you have to decide. You're the one who knows your own situation and how much you can afford. You need to look at what God has given you and then give out of your own sense of gratitude.

MR. BEAN: That sounds great, but it doesn't tell me how much I should give. How much do you give?

PASTOR GIVENS: That's a pretty personal question, Greg. Besides, what I give doesn't really have much to do with what you give. We're in different income brackets and have different financial situations. I'll tell you this. We've started to tithe. We didn't use to. But a few years back, we made a commitment to grow in our giving and we've been increasing our gift by one percent of our annual income each year until now, this year, for the first time, we are giving ten percent.

MR. BEAN: Ten percent! According to last year's annual report, you are making about $40,000 a year. You mean you are giving $4,000 a year to the church? Why, that's over $80 a week!

PASTOR GIVENS: You're really quick with numbers. I guess being an accountant helps that way. But, actually, that's not what we are giving.

MR. BEAN: So, you're not really giving ten percent then?

PASTOR GIVENS: No, my wife also works and we tithe on her income, too. But our whole tithe doesn't go to this church. We give to the seminary and to the local emergency food shelf and a few other favorite charities as well. But, Community of Hope does get the biggest portion of our tithe.

MR. BEAN: So, if your wife makes even $15,000 a year, that's another $30 a week. You mean to tell me you're giving away $110 a week!

PASTOR GIVENS: Are you this quick when it comes to figuring out income tax, too?

MR. BEAN: If you are giving $110 a week, then you're giving $100 a week more than I am!

PASTOR GIVENS: *(pause)* What do you want me to say?

MR. BEAN: Why don't you let people know what you give? That would demonstrate some leadership.

PASTOR GIVENS: I guess I've always been afraid that would sound like I was bragging. We each have to decide what we will give. There are people who give more than I do — both dollarwise and percentage wise — I know some people who give 20 percent of their income away. There are also people who give less.

MR. BEAN: I wouldn't consider it bragging. I would welcome it as an example to follow.

PASTOR GIVENS: I'll think about that. Meanwhile, if you want to figure out what to give, why not make a commitment to grow in your giving? Figure out what percentage of your income you are giving now and commit yourself to increasing your gift by one percent of your household income each year until you reach a tithe or double tithe or whatever your personal goal for giving might be?

MR. BEAN: Do most people tithe?

PASTOR GIVENS: I'm sure they don't. In fact, our church council figured out that if our congregation gave just five percent of their total income, we would have to spend as much time figuring out the best ways to expand the budget as we currently do figuring ways to cut it.

MR. BEAN: So, why do you tithe?

PASTOR GIVENS: Two reasons, I guess. It is a biblical benchmark. It's what the Bible suggests we give as a starting point. The other reason is it gives us joy. My wife and I have discovered that the things we are able to do for others are the things that make us happiest. There's a real joy in giving.

MR. BEAN: Well, why don'tcha tell people about the joy of giving?

PASTOR GIVENS: I think I've tried. I've certainly mentioned it in sermons and stewardship letters enough times.

MR. BEAN: I guess when you've talked about money I've just tuned you out. It seems like the church is always asking for money.

PASTOR GIVENS: If people gave more generously and more sacrificially, the church wouldn't have to ask for money.

MR. BEAN: And people would find a lot more joy in giving, too. Right? I guess if our gifts really were a reflection of our gratitude for God's grace and love, we'd give more generously and we'd find more joy in it.

PASTOR GIVENS: Right. Say, what brought this whole conversation about, anyway?

MR. BEAN: Oh, Dan was doing a school project on money management and was asking questions about what we spend on various things. He pointed out that our gift to the church was one of our smallest expenses. I guess that got me thinking. Now that I have talked to you, I'll have to do some more thinking.

PASTOR GIVENS: And praying. It always helps to ask God for guidance as you decide what you should give. It shouldn't be just an economic decision. It should be a commitment to give in a way that shows God your joy and thanksgiving for all he has given. In fact, let's say a prayer of thanks right now.

MR. BEAN: That would be great.

PASTOR GIVENS: O God, we give you thanks for all your gifts. We thank you for creating us and sustaining us. Mostly, we thank you for giving us the gift of your Son. He gave up his life for our sake. Be with Greg and his family and all the families of our church as they decide what they should give as a sign of their gratitude to you. Help them to make it a generous gift — a gift that will bring them great joy. In Jesus' name we pray. Amen.

— The End —

WHY DO WE BAPTIZE?

Cast of Characters:

JOHN HEDSTROM: Outgoing student, not afraid to speak his mind or ask questions.
DON GARCIA: John's best friend.
JENNY WISE: Smartest kid in the class and knows it. Has lots of good answers, but can be a little snobbish about her knowledge.
MATT KNOWLES: A bit quieter and more reserved than the other two boys.
KIM WONG: Participates in the discussion but, unlike Jenny, she doesn't have all the answers.
MRS. PHILIPS: The teacher.

Setting:

A modern day Sunday school classroom. Upper elementary age students are sitting in their classroom. When JOHN enters, he sits down by DON and the dialogue begins.

JOHN: Didja go to church yet?

DON: No, we're goin' to second service.

JOHN: There was a baptism this morning. Don'tcha you just hate it when there's a baptism?

JENNY: I like baptisms. I think they're neat.

JOHN: Why? What's to like about 'em?

JENNY: Well, the babies look so cute, all dressed up in their baptismal gowns and I think it's fun when the pastor holds them and introduces them to the congregation. It makes everyone in the church smile. Babies make people feel good.

DON: I think it's funny when the pastor is holding 'em and they start to cry. He gives 'em back to their parents pretty quick when they start squawking.

MATT: My baby brother screamed through the whole service when he was baptized — the pastor was hollering to be heard over him, but mostly you heard Bobby bawling away.

KIM: That's nothing! When my little cousin was baptized last year, her diaper leaked and she wet all over her mother's dress!

(All laugh except Jenny)

JENNY: Gross! You guys are really gross!

MRS. PHILIPS: Hi, class. What are you discussing?

JENNY: Oh, we're just talking about baptism.

MRS. PHILIPS: You were? Well, let's talk about it some more. Do you have any particular questions about it?

JOHN: I do. Why do they hafta to have baptisms during church? It makes the service so much longer. Why can't they just have the family there for it?

MRS. PHILIPS: What do you kids think?

JENNY: I think it's because that baby is our brother or sister.

JOHN: No way. I'm not having any more brothers or sisters! Besides, no brother of mine would bawl like that little kid did today!

JENNY: *(sarcastically)* Oh, I 'spose they'd be quiet and perfect like you! I didn't mean they'd be a brother or sister that lives in your house. I meant like what the pastor says about welcoming this person into the church family and relating to them as a brother or sister in Christ.

MRS. PHILIPS: I think you're absolutely right, Jenny. Part of what happens in baptism is that the child becomes a member of the church. So, we should be there to witness the baptism and welcome them into our congregation. What else happens in baptism?

DON: The pastor pours waters over the kid's head. Why does he do that anyway?

MRS. PHILIPS: It's symbolic. Do you know what we mean when we say something is symbolic?

DON: It means it stands for something else. It's meant to remind you of something else.

MRS. PHILIPS: What's pouring water on a baby's head supposed to stand for or remind you of?

KIM: It reminds me of giving a kid a bath or at least washing their hair.

MRS. PHILIPS: That's right. We talk about our sins being washed away in baptism.

JOHN: Hold it a minute! How can a little baby have sins that need washing away? He isn't old enough to have done anything wrong. I mean, I'm eleven and I've hardly done anything wrong!

ALL: *(Groan and moan)* Awww!

JOHN: No, but a baby hasn't had time to be sinful.

MRS. PHILIPS: Well, John, sin isn't just doing bad things. We talk about sin being a state or a condition. Have you ever heard the words, "original sin?" Original sin means we are born in a state of separation from God. It isn't like we are born perfect people and then we start sinning and become imperfect. We are born imperfect. Because Adam and Eve sinned, everyone born since then inherited sin from them.

When we are born, we have lots of needs. We need food, clothing, and people to take care of us, otherwise we would die. We also need a relationship with God. God gives us that relationship through baptism. He washes away our sins, even our original sin, and adopts us as his children.

KIM: I have a question. If Jesus was God's son and he was sinless, then why did he need to be baptized?

JENNY: I think I know. He did it as an example for us. He did it to show us that we should be baptized.

MRS. PHILIPS: That's right.

MATT: But something different happened at Jesus' baptism. The Bible talks about the Holy Spirit descending upon Jesus like a dove. What was that all about?

MRS. PHILIPS: That was a sign showing people who Jesus was. It also tells us that we receive the gift of the Holy Spirit in Baptism.

DON: How do we know we have the Holy Spirit in us?

JENNY: Because we have faith. The Holy Spirit gives us the gift of faith. Without the Holy Spirit, we can't have faith.

JOHN: How come you know so much?

JENNY: Because unlike some people, I listen in church!

MATT: Tell me about godparents. I know they stand up there and watch the baby get baptized, but why? What else do they do?

JOHN: I saw a video once called "The Godfather." It was radical. I mean the godfather had all these people killed. There was blood and guts everywhere!

JENNY: Just the kind of movie you would like!

JOHN: I did like it!

DON: So did I!

MRS. PHILIPS: That movie didn't have much of anything to do with what we talk about as godparents in baptism. He was a godfather to a baby, but he certainly wasn't living out his promises as a sponsor.

KIM: What promises are those?

JENNY: I know. Godparents or sponsors promise to pray for the baby. They also promise to adopt it if the parents die.

MRS. PHILIPS: Well, the praying part is right, but the adoption part or being the child's guardian isn't necessarily true. That's something the parents would have to specify in their will. Sponsors are people who say they will help the parents fulfill the promises they make in baptism. What things do the parents and sponsors promise to do to raise their child in the faith?

JOHN: Teach them the Ten Commandments.

DON: And the creed;

MATT: And the Lord's Prayer.

KIM: Teach them to pray and read the Bible.

MATT: Bring them to church and Sunday school?

JENNY: Be an example to them.

MRS. PHILIPS: Good. All of those things are true. And if the parents don't do them or stop doing those things, it's up to the sponsors to remind them of what they promised.

JOHN: I've got another question. What if a baby dies before it gets baptized? Does it go, you know — *(Pointing and looking down)* — down there?

MRS. PHILIPS: What do you think?

JOHN: I don't think so. I mean it wasn't the kid's fault he didn't get baptized!

MRS. PHILIPS: The way our church looks at it, God is a gracious and loving God. He gives us the gift of baptism so we can know for sure that we belong to him. But he isn't going to say to some little baby, "I'm sorry, but your parents didn't manage to get you baptized, so you can't come into heaven." We're saved not by what we do, but by what Jesus Christ did for us on the cross. There's a Bible passage, Mark 16:16, that says something to us about this. It says: "Whoever believes and is baptized will be saved; whoever does not believe will be condemned." Notice it doesn't say whoever isn't baptized is condemned, but whoever does not believe.

JENNY: So, baptism is a gift to us. A way that God shows us we belong to him. He washes away our sins, adopts us into his family and gives us the gift of the Holy Spirit. It seems to me baptism is awfully important. I don't think you should complain about something as important as that, John Hedstrom.

JOHN: I guess I've always looked at it as something taking extra time instead of looking at how important it is for the baby.

KIM: And for all of us. After all, that baby is becoming a member of our family!

(*Bell rings)

MATT: Say, we spent our whole class time talking about baptism. What were we going to study about today anyway?

MRS. PHILIPS: Baptism!

(All laugh)

MRS. PHILIPS: Let's close with a prayer.

O God, we give you thanks for the gift of baptism. We thank you that because of this sacrament we have a concrete sign that our sins are forgiven and that you have claimed us as your own. Let your Holy Spirit cause our faith to grow so that we may always live out the promises our parents made for us in this sacrament.   Amen.

— The End —

*You will need to recruit someone to ring the Sunday school bell.

WHY DO WE COMMUNE?

A drama for Lutheran Churches

Cast of Characters:

    PASTOR BARBARA BORNER: Late 50s, articulate, knowledgeable.
    NED ABRAHMSON: Early 50s, rather angry, opinionated, doesn't like change, wants things done his way.
    ALICE NEWTON: Mid 40s, mother of three, intelligent, open minded.
    WILMA LEATHERMAN: Late 40s, concerned, questioning.
    BOB NEWELL: Fifth grade boy, outgoing, questioning.
    LIZ ABRAHMSON: Fifth grade girl, Ned's daughter.
    JERRY NEWTON: Fifth grade boy, Alice's son.
    LYNDELL LEATHERMAN: Fifth grade boy.
    JOAN NEWELL: Mid 30s, sensitive, insightful, Bob's mother.

Setting:

Early communion class. Chairs in a semicircle. Pastor stands. You can have a blackboard or flip chart up front to make it look like a classroom, if you like.

PASTOR: Welcome to our early communion instruction class.

Rather than start right in on the materials, I'd like to know if any of you have any praticular questions about communion. That way, we can get right to the heart of your concerns.

NED: I've got a question. I don't quite understand why we changed things. When I was a kid, you couldn't take communion until you were confirmed. Now, these kids in fifth grade are invited to take communion after this class. What was wrong with the old way?

PASTOR: The old way was not necessarily wrong, but this way is right for our time. Alice, you were on the committee that studied the question of early communion. Can you share some of the reasons for change that were meaningful to you and to the group?

ALICE: We studied this issue for a long time. One thing that sticks in my mind is that holy communion is a sacrament. It's God's gift to us. He shares himself with us in the bread and wine, and that isn't something we earn. We could never earn that — not by attending two years of classes, not by being confirmed, not by doing anything. Withholding the sacrament until a person is confirmed smacks of earning the right to receive it.

PASTOR: That's an important reason for me, too. Another thing I think is important is that these fifth graders are old enough to learn and understand the significance of the sacrament. If we're worried about people receiving the sacrament in the right spirit, I believe they are at the right age.

ALICE: I know when we first offered these classes, my John was in seventh grade and Jim was in fifth grade. John kept talking about getting to drink the wine, while Jim had a more mature attitude. He was excited about being able to share in the sacrament with us. That seemed to be Jerry's attitude too when we talked about taking communion on our way up to this class today.

NED: Do you think these children, or any children, age 10 or 11, are prepared to take the sacrament? I mean, St. Paul seems pretty emphatic about the importance of examining yourself before receiving the sacrament. He even says if you don't recognize the meaning of the Lord's body when you eat the bread and drink the cup, then you bring judgment on yourself.

PASTOR: In our class, we'll take a look at 1 Corinthians 11, where Paul talks about the Lord's Supper. Since you brought it up, however, let me give you a little background on that situation. The Corinthian church had what they called "agape meals" or "love feasts." It would be a bit like our potlucks. Everyone brought food to share. Their whole church, which Paul defines as the body of Christ, gathered to eat together and share in the sacrament.

The problem was, the rich people sat together over in their corner of the room and ate caviar and the fancy foods they brought, while the poor people sat in another corner and ate their meager crusts of bread. St. Paul really gets after the Corinthians for allowing this division. He says that because they are failing to recognize the needs of the poor and their unity as a church family, they are failing to recognize the body of Christ. Therefore, they are eating and drinking judgment onto themselves.

ALICE: I remember that Martin Luther had a good definition of what's required for a person to be rightly prepared or ready to receive the sacrament. The problem is, I don't remember what it was.

PASTOR: Do you mean what he says in the small catechism? "That a person is well prepared and worthy who believes these words, 'Given and shed for you for the remission of sins.'"

ALICE: That's it. I knew it didn't require anything very complicated.

WILMA: I have a concern about communion. I am a teetotaler. I have seen too many people ruin their lives with alcohol. Why don't we use grape juice instead of wine for holy communion?

PASTOR: I suppose because Jesus used wine.

WILMA: Well, like I have said before, that is the one thing I don't like about Jesus!

LYNDELL: I have gone to the Catholic church with my friend Chris. They don't even get the wine there, just the bread — why is that?

PASTOR: That goes way back in history to the Fourth Lateran Council in 1215 A.D. That council discussed the fact that they believed when the priest blessed the bread and the wine it became the body and blood of Christ.
   The wine was easy to spill and they didn't want to run the risk of spilling the blood of Christ. They decided that the priest should drink the cup for everyone and that the rest of the congregation would only receive the bread. However, there are many Roman Catholic churches that now offer the wine to all those who desire to receive it. Through our ecumenical dialogues we are discovering that Lutheran theology and Roman Catholic theology have many more things in common than we once believed. As we talk and understand each other more, we find many common elements of faith.

LYNDELL: Well, what do Lutherans believe about the bread and the wine?

WILMA: We just believe it **represents** the body and blood of Christ. Right, Pastor?

PASTOR: Well, it isn't easy to explain, but it isn't just that the bread and wine **represent** Christ's body and blood. They are not just symbols. In the Lutheran church, we talk about "The Real Presence." We believe that Christ is actually present in the sacrament. He comes to us in, with and under the bread and wine. He is present for us in the sacrament in a special way.

LIZ: You mean we are actually eating his flesh and drinking his blood? Ish! That sounds gross! I saw a movie once where people ate other people. They were called cannonballs or something.

PASTOR: Not cannonballs, cannibals. But, no, Liz, we are not cannibals. We don't digest Christ like we digest the bread and wine. Instead of us digesting or changing Christ, he comes into us and changes us. He transforms us. He comes to us in communion to strengthen our faith and empower us for life.

LIZ: How can he do that? I don't understand.

PASTOR: I can't really explain it full either. It is a mystery. God doesn't tell us the whys and hows of lots of things. He is beyond our understanding and we can't always comprehend his ways. But he asks us to accept things in faith. Even though we don't understand everything about holy communion and Christ's presence in the sacrament, we can still benefit from it.

ALICE: I remember in our study to decide about early communion, we talked about it being a mystery. Someone said electricity is a mystery, too. No one completely understands it, and yet we can benefit from turning on a light switch, even though we don't know all about how electricity works. We don't have to know how Christ is present to believe he is there. After all, he said he would be when he said, "This is my body. This is my blood."

JERRY: I have always wondered why we talk about "celebrating" holy communion. Everyone always looks so serious. It doesn't look much like a celebration. Are we supposed to be happy, or sad, or what?

PASTOR: I believe it's a combination of both, Jerry. In holy communion, we remember that Christ's body was broken for us and his blood was shed. And yet, we can celebrate the fact that he loved us enough to sacrifice himself for us. In the confession and absolution, we have already received the assurance of the forgiveness of our sins. Now, in holy communion, we have a tangible, visible reminder of that forgiveness of our sins.

ALICE: We also talk about it as a foretaste of the feast to come. I certainly expect heaven to be a happy place — a place filled with smiles and laughter. The heavenly feast won't be people sitting around with sad looks on their faces. It'll be a celebration.

BOB: How often should a person take holy communion?

PASTOR: In the early Christian church, people celebrated holy communion every day. In the early Lutheran church, in fact, for the first 300 years of its existence, we had every Sunday communion.

NED: What changed things then? My father told me they would only have communion once or twice a year when he was growing up.

PASTOR: Things changed because of the pietist movement, a movement in Scandinavia and Germany, in the 1700s. It goes back to what you said earlier about St. Paul telling the Corinthians to make sure they were rightly prepared and worthy. The leaders of the pietist movement said that religion was empty and that it needed to affect a person's everyday life more. They suggested that if you sinned, you were not worthy of receiving the sacrament, so people stopped communing. They didn't want to eat and drink damnation unto themselves. Now, I believe, we have regained a proper perspective and realize that it is precisely because we sin that we need holy communion to assure us of God's forgiveness and give us strength to renew our lives.

BOB: That still doesn't tell me how often we should go to communion.

PASTOR: I don't think there is a magic number, Bob. I personally commune every time it is offered.

NED: Won't you run the risk of it becoming meaningless if you commune all the time? I mean, that would take the specialness away from it for me.

JOAN: Not for me. Communion has become more and more meaningful to me through the years. I guess that's why I am so anxious for Bob to be able to receive holy communion. It's really an intimate time of communication between myself and God and between myself and other Christians. God speaks to me in this meal, telling me I'm a forgiven person, a person who will live with him forever because Christ suffered and died to save me. Even though we don't talk at the communion table, I'm in communion with other members of the church because we share in this holy meal together. I'm excited about sharing it with Bob.

LIZ: You said people don't talk at communion, but some people do. I hear some people say, "Amen" when they receive the bread and wine. Why do they do that?

PASTOR: When we say, "Amen," Liz, we are saying, "Yes, it shall be so" or "Yes, I believe this." When you are handed the bread and hear the words, "This is the body of Christ given for you," it is proper to say "Amen," for you are saying, "Yes, I believe that this is Christ's body."

Does anyone else have any other burning questions? *(Pause)* If not, let's take a ten-minute break before we start looking at the regular material for our early communion class.

— The End —

WHY DO WE COMMUNE?

A drama for Non-Lutheran congregations

Cast of Characters:

    RUTH UTZMAN: Mid to late 30s, Don's wife. Mother of Tim and Tina.
    DON UTZMAN: Mid to late 30s, Ruth's husband. Father of Tim and Tina.
    TIM UTZMAN: Sixth-grade boy — questioning, curious.
    TINA UTZMAN: Third-grade girl — independent, outgoing.

Setting:

The setting is Utzman's kitchen. Ruth is preparing lunch when Tim enters asking about lunch. Props might include a table that serves as a kitchen counter with a cutting board, knife and other items that might be part of lunch preparation.

TIM: Hey, when's lunch? I'm starved.

RUTH: I would guess in about half an hour. You can help by setting the table.

TIM: Aw, Mom, do I hafta?

RUTH: Yes, you "hafta."

TIM: Could I have a snack first? I'm about to faint.

RUTH: I don't want you to spoil your lunch by eating stuff now.

TIM: I won't spoil my lunch. Besides, you and Dad had something to eat at the church and I didn't.

RUTH: Oh, you mean communion.

TIM: Yeah, why do they have communion anyway? Part of the reason I'm so hungry is church went in ta overtime 'causa communion.

RUTH: Well, it's a very important meal.

(Don enters as Ruth is saying this)

DON: Every meal is important — especially this one — I'm starved, when do we eat?

RUTH: We'll eat as soon as things are ready. You can help things along by cleaning the broccoli.

TIM: Broccoli — you gotta be kidding. Can't we have somethin' else? I'm starved, but I'm not starved enough to eat broccoli.

(Tina enters)

TINA: We're having broccoli? Oh gross!

RUTH: I'm glad you're all so pleased with the vegetable selection. Maybe you'd like to plan the meals from now on.

TINA: Yeah, I'll do it. We'll have pizza on Monday; McDonalds on Tuesday; Kentucky Fried on Wednesday, macaroni and cheese on Thursday; and Friday we'll go out. How does that sound?

RUTH: Like way too much junk food. No, we need to eat balanced meals to stay healthy and vegetables are part of a well-balanced meal.

Don, just before you came in Tim was asking about holy communion and why we have it.

DON: Oh, that's the important meal you were talking about. Well, your mom is right, Tim. Holy communion is a very important meal.

TIM: Why? What's so special about it?

DON: Well, for one thing, it's a sacrament. Holy communion and holy baptism are the two sacraments in the church.

TINA: What's a sack-a-mint?

DON: Sacrament, Tina. It's a special rite of the church. Something that Jesus instructed us to do.

RUTH: Jesus told us to baptize so that people would be brought into God's family. He told us to share in holy communion to remember that he died for our sins.

TIM: How does somethin' to eat remind us of forgiveness?

DON: Do you remember the story of the last supper that Jesus had with his disciples? It took place on what we call Maundy Thursday. He was arrested later that night and then tried and sentenced to be crucified on Good Friday. At that meal, he took some bread and said "This is my body which is broken for you. Do this in memory of me." Then he gave them a cup of wine and said "This cup is God's new covenant sealed with my blood. Whenever you drink it do so in memory of me." Jesus commands us to share this meal in memory of him.

TIM: But why? Can't we remember him without a meal that makes church go so long?

RUTH: Well, I suppose we could. In fact we do on Sundays when we don't have holy communion. But this is a special way of remembering. A more meaningful way. It's like the difference between saying "I love you" and both saying and doing something that really shows that love.

DON: It's like a visible, tangible reminder of what Jesus has done for us. Maybe this will help. Both your mother and I wear wedding rings. We tell each other that we love one another and that is really important. But my wedding ring is a tangible visible reminder that I am loved and that I am married.

TIM: Dad, that doesn't have much to do with a meal reminding you that you're forgiven.

RUTH: Well, think of it this way. Every day I'm glad you were born.

DON: *(Interrupts)* Well, most days at least.

RUTH: No, every day — even the bad days. Every day I am glad that you are born. But on your birthday we have a special meal and a party to celebrate the event. That meal and party make it a special celebration of your birth. In the same way, we celebrate God's love and forgiveness every day, but holy communion makes the celebration more special and more meaningful.

DON: Your birthday party illustration is a good one, Ruth. It reminds me of another important dimension of holy communion. When you have a birthday party, other people come and celebrate with you. Your birthday would be a lot less exciting if you just celebrated it all alone. Well, holy communion is a meal we celebrate with other people too. It is a meal we share with God, but also with other Christians.

RUTH: Holy communion reminds us of our unity as Christians. Just as we share in this one bread and one cup so we share in one common faith.

DON: So holy communion really is an important meal Tim. It helps us to realize what Jesus did for us on the cross and how he died so our sins could be forgiven. The bread and wine are concrete reminders — they make it more real.

RUTH: And the fact that we commune with other Christians reminds us that we are united in faith with them.

TIM: I guess it is a pretty important meal. When can I start taking holy communion?

TINA: Yeah, I want to, too.

RUTH: We'll have to talk about that some more. Since we are new to this church we'll have to discuss it with the pastor. Some churches want you to be confirmed before you receive communion. Others leave it up to the discretion of the parent. Would you like to start taking communion?

TIM: Yeah, I think it would mean more to me if I could be involved in it instead of just watchin' you guys take it. I'd like to take communion.

TINA: So would I, but first I'd like to eat lunch. Can we do that pretty soon?

RUTH: We'll do it as soon as the table is set and the vegetable is done, and as soon as you kids have clean hands. Why don't you go wash up?

(lights dim — cast exits)

— The End —

WHY DO WE CONFIRM OUR FAITH?

Cast of Characters:

    GEORGE LEWIS: Ninth-grade boy — doesn't go to church. Interested in horror movies and girls.

    PETE JOHNSON: Ninth-grade boy — has mixed emotions about confirmation and church.

    MARY EDWARDS: Ninth-grade girl — enthusiastic about confirmation.

    TONY PEREZ: Ninth-grade boy — dislikes confirmation classes. Plans to drop out of church after confirmation.

    BARB WILLIAMS: Ninth-grade girl — dislikes confirmation. Her parents force her to be involved.

    MR. LINK: School teacher. Wants to teach the students about the meaning of confirmation.

    HUA CHING: Ninth-grade boy — articulte, serious about confirmation and its importance.

Setting:

The halls at school. Students should have books and/or book bags. Enter by walking up the center or side aisle.

GEORGE: Say, Pete, d'ya'wanna go to a movie with me on Sunday afternoon? "The Slime Creature" is playing at Cinema 8.

PETE: I'd like to, but I can't. I'm gettin' confirmed that day.

GEORGE: Confirmed! What's that?

PETE: Somethin' at church. You publicly affirm your baptismal vows during a worship service.

GEORGE: Do you hafta give a speech or somethin' in fronta the whole church?

PETE: I sure hope not! No one said anything about that. Usually the whole class just says the creed and stuff as a group and answers some questions with "I do" or somethin' like that.

GEORGE: Sounds like a wedding. You said the whole class — who else is in your class?

PETE: Mary Edwards, Tony Perez, Barb Williams, Hua Ching, Chris Stewart, Jan Peterson.

GEORGE: Jan Peterson! Really? I'd go to classes justa sit and look at her!

(Enter Tony Perez)

TONY: Hi, guys. What's happenin?

PETE: Hi, Tony. George says he'd go to confirmation justa look at Jan Peterson.

TONY: No way! Nobody's that good looking. Do you know how long we've been goin' to confirmation classes, George? Two years! Every Wednesday night for **two** years!

GEORGE; Man, that is a long time. Wha'da'ya do in there?

TONY: Nothin', it's boring. You hafta memorize a buncha junk and take sermon notes and tests. It's the pits.

GEORGE: Memorize! Wha'da'ya hafta memorize?

(Mary Edwards approaches from off stage)

PETE: Oh, like the creed and the Lord's Prayer and the books of the Bible. Ask Mary, she knows all that stuff. Hey, Mary, come'ere. George here wants ta know all about confirmation.

MARY: Isn't it exciting? I can hardly wait for Sunday. Are you gonna come to our confirmation service, George?

GEORGE: I dunno. Is Jan Peterson gonna be there?

PETE: You've got Jan Peterson on the brain. There's Barb Williams — she's in the class, too. Barb, did you ever get your memory work turned in so you can get confirmed on Sunday?

(Enter Barb Williams)

BARB; Yeah, whata hassle. Mom made me stay home all weekend 'til I got it all done. I don't even care if I get confirmed, but my parents are makin' me. They said if I can't be responsible enough to get this stuff done, then I wouldn't be responsible enough for them to trust me with a car when I get old enough to get my license.

PETE: That's crazy. What does confirmation have to do with driving a car?

(Enter Mr. Link)

MR. LINK: Hi, kids. What — does Barb think she's getting a car for a confirmation present?

BARB: Don't I wish! No, my parents are hanging confirmation over my head like a club! They said unless I get my memory work done, I couldn't get my license when I turned sixteen.

MR. LINK: Well, did you get it all done?

BARB: Yeah, but it ruined my whole weekend.

TONY: Just think though, after this next weekend all your weekends'll be free. After confirmation we won't hafta go to church anymore.

MR. LINK: But, that's just the opposite of what confirmation is all about. When you get confirmed, you're promising to worship, learn and serve. Pastor Joyner has said over and over again that confirmation isn't a graduation from church, it's a commitment to greater involvement in the church.

PETE: That sounds good, but how do we get more involved? I mean, what'll they let us do? Adults run the church. You can't do anything more after you're confirmed than you can now.

MR. LINK: Of course you can. Once you're confirmed, you can vote at congregational meetings; you can be part of the senior high youth group; you can help with Sunday school or Bible school; there's lots of stuff you can do.

TONY: I, for one, will be glad I don't hafta go to Sunday school anymore. I'm sick of classes.

PETE: Yeah, me too. Goin' to confirmation class was enough for me.

MR. LINK: Aren't you going to the senior high class or the forums at church?

MARY: I'm planning on going.

PETE: You would. You're so smart you probably like going to all that class stuff.

MARY: I did enjoy confirmation class. I mean, parts of it were boring, but I learned a lot, too.

BARB: Like what?

MARY: I thought it was neat when we discussed that Apostles' Creed and talked about what we believed. I liked what Pastor Joyner said about doubts and questions being okay because they can motivate us to learn and grow in our faith.

MR. LINK: As I understand it, part of what you're committing yourself to on confirmation day is continued learning.

TONY: What else is there to learn? I mean, after all, we just spent two years studying all that stuff.

MR. LINK: Tony, there are people who spend years in seminary studying full time and they still don't know everything there is to know about God.

BARB: Well, they want to be preachers, I sure don't. I don't even like going to church, but my folks make me.

MR. LINK: I need to attend worship in order to keep growing in my faith.

MARY: Me, too. Taking sermon notes really helped me to learn how to listen to the sermon and going to communion is really important to me.

PETE: Sermon notes! That's somethin' I won't miss. But you're right. I never used to listen until I had to start taking notes. Pastor Joyner does have interesting sermons most of the time.

MR. LINK: I almost always get something out of the worship service, even if it's just confessing my sins and hearing that I'm forgiven. It's essential to keep growing in the faith. It's pretty hard to face adult problems with an adolescent faith.

(Enter Hua Ching)

HUA: Sounds like some pretty serious discussion here. What're you guys talking about?

MARY: Confirmation. Tony, Pete and Barb don't seem to think they'll need to attend any more classes at church after confirmation. I think they figure they know it all.

HUA: Sure, we've all learned a lot in confirmation class, but we all have a lot more to learn. You guys are jocks. You know what would happen to your bod if you stopped eating and exercising. It would deteriorate. The same is true of our spiritual life. If we don't feed our faith and put it to work, it deteriorates also.

BARB: Maybe so, but I can't see going to any more classes, at least not for a while.

MR. LINK: Why? Confirmation classes weren't that bad, were they?

BARB: I enjoyed the spitball fights.

PETE: I thought it was fun when we hid all the erasers and Pastor Joyner had to use a dishtowel to clean the blackboard.

MARY: There were other things that were good, too. I thought we had some helpful discussions on lots of topics. I think I'll miss confirmation classes.

PETE: Not me!

BARB: Not me either!

TONY: No way!

HUA: I might miss the classes a little, but I'm really looking forward to getting confirmed. That's going to be a special day.

BARB: Well, I'm looking forward to the presents. My brother made a haul. He got over $200, plus lots of neat stuff.

MR. LINK: I hope it means more to you than just presents, Barb. I think you'll really be missing out on something if that's all it means.

BARB: Like what?

MR. LINK: Like a chance to stand in front of the whole congregation and state your faith, saying, "This is what I believe and this is the faith that will guide my life."

MARY: And like making a commitment to be an active member of the church.

HUA: And like publicly promising to try and grow in the faith and serve God through the church.

PETE: Maybe so. I do know one thing. I'll be glad when it's over. Say, George, do you wanna come and see us get confirmed?

GEORGE: I dunno. It's going to be a tough choice between coming to see you guys and Jan Peterson or going to see "The Slime Creature."

BARB: Maybe you can do both. You can come and see us and then save yourself three bucks on the movie and just look in the mirror!

ALL: *(Laugh)*

— The End —

WHY DO WE WORSHIP SO OFTEN?

A drama for Maundy Thursday

Cast of Characters:

    PETE WILLIAMS: A young boy 10 to 13 years old. Strong willed and questioning.
    BILL WILLIAMS: Father in the family. Early 40s.
    CAROL WILLIAMS: Mother in the family. Early 40s.
    ALICE WILLIAMS: Pete's 16- or 17-year-old sister.

Setting:

The Williams' living room on Monday evening of Holy Week. Bill Williams is seated reading the paper when his son, Pete, enters.

PETE: Say, Dad, guess what?

BILL: What?

PETE: We have a spring break — there's no school Thursday or Friday.

BILL: They call it spring break now, huh? When I was a kid, they used to call it Easter break.

PETE: Why'do'ya suppose they changed it? It **will** be Easter next Sunday.

BILL: I suppose it's only right — not everyone in the school is Christian and therefore, they wouldn't celebrate Easter. They don't take breaks for Jewish holidays like Hanukkah or Rosh Hashanah and we Christians wouldn't be too excited if they called spring break "Passover vacation."

PETE: Well, spring break, Easter break, or whatever, I was wondering if I could have some friends sleep over on Thursday night.

BILL: I'm afraid not, son, that's Maundy Thursday.

PETE: Not Monday through Thursday — just Thursday and Friday.

BILL: No, I said it was **Maundy** Thursday.

PETE: What are you talking about? Monday is Monday and Thursday is Thursday! I've never heard of Monday Thursday.

BILL: Not Monday, Pete, Maundy. M-A-U-N-D-Y — Maundy.

PETE: So, what does Maundy mean?

BILL: To tell the truth, I don't remember. But, I do know it's a part of Holy Week and we have a worship service to go to.

PETE: You mean we're going to church on Thursday night! A Thursday night when there is no school! What for? I mean we've been goin' Wednesdays and Sundays and now we're goin' on Thursday, too?

BILL: *(Stands up)* Calm down, we aren't going Wednesday. The Wednesday Lenten services are over. This is Holy Week, and so we'll be going to Maundy Thursday services.

PETE: *(Interrupts)* What for? You don't even know what Maundy Thursday means. Why do we hafta go when we don't even know what the service is for?

CAROL: What's all the commotion about? What are you two arguing about now?

PETE: I wanted to have some friends over on Thursday because there is no school and Dad says we are goin' to some dumb Monday-Thursday thing at church. He can't even tell me what Monday-Thursday is all about!

CAROL: It's Maundy, dear, not Monday, and it's a very important day in Holy Week. It's a time when we remember Jesus' Last Supper with his disciples.

PETE: So, is that what Maundy means — the Last Supper?

CAROL: No, I think it means "commandment." At the Last Supper Jesus washed the disciples' feet and then he gave them a commandment. He said, "Love one another. As I have loved you, so you must love one another."
   (Calls upstairs) Alice, will you bring your dictionary down here?
   (Speaks to Pete again) Let's look it up and see for sure what it means.
   (Alice enters carrying dictionary)

ALICE: What, are you guys playing Scrabble or do ya just want to settle another family argument? *(Hands dictionary to mother)*

CAROL: *(Looks in dictionary)* We're not having an argument. Pete was just asking what the word Maundy means.

ALICE: You don't know that? Whatta "stup." Monday is the first day of the week.

PETE: We're talking about Maundy — M-A-U-N-D-Y — as in Maundy Thursday. And, besides, Monday is the second day of the week. What a jerk!

BILL: That's enough, you two! Try to be a little civil to each other.

CAROL: Here it is. "Maundy" — the religious ceremony of washing the feet of others in commemoration of the washing of the disciples' feet by Christ at the Last Supper. Maundatur — command; from the use of the command at the beginning of the ceremony." So, Maundy does mean command — from the new commandment Jesus gave his disciples.

ALICE: Since you dragged me down here away from my homework, now's as good a time as any to ask you. Can I have the car Friday night? A bunch of us wanna go to the movies.

CAROL: Not this Friday, Alice. This Friday is Good Friday. We will be going to church.

PETE: Are you serious? Ya mean, we're goin' to go to church Wednesday, Thursday, and Friday? We could just as well set the camper up in the parking lot!

BILL: Not Wednesday, Pete. I already told you that Wednesday Lenten services are over. This is Holy Week.

ALICE: It sounds like a holy week. If we go to church that much, we will be so holy nobody'll be able to stand us!

CAROL: Just a minute, here. I think you two need to reevaluate your priorities a little and think about what's important. I don't think it's out of line to ask you to go to a couple of extra worship services once a year to offer thanks to God for sending Jesus into the world to save us.

BILL: There are some churches that have Easter Vigil services. They have people going to church Thursday night, Friday night, Saturday night and and Easter Sunday morning.

PETE: What on earth for?

ALICE: I think it's to make you pay for your sins — all in one weekend! It's like grounding you for religious reasons!

PETE: For once we see somethin' the same way!

CAROL: And you're both wrong! God has given us a great gift. On Maundy Thursday we remember his new commandment to love one another and we celebrate holy communion just as Jesus celebrated it with his disciples at his Last Supper. On Good Friday we go to worship to reflect on the fact that he died for our sins. And, on Easter Sunday we rejoice in the resurrection.

ALICE: It still sounds like a lotta church to me.

BILL: And you two sound pretty ungrateful to me! I don't think a couple of extra worship services is too much to ask as an expression of our thanks to God for the sacrifices he made for us.

CAROL: Well, that isn't all God asks for though. He asks for our lives. Our response isn't just to attend a few worship services. Our response is to live out our love for God in our everyday lives.

BILL: Why don't we settle on a compromise here? Pete, you could invite your friends to go to worship with us and then stay over. That would be a good witness to them about what we believe.

PETE: Is that the service where they turn out all the lights? That one's kinda cool.

CAROL: No, that's the Good Friday Tenebrae service, but if you would rather have them stay over after the Good Friday service, that would be fine with me.

ALICE: What about me? When can I have the car to go to the movies?

BILL: That's up to you — you could either go to the Saturday afternoon show or you could plan on next Friday night.

ALICE: Why not Saturday night?

CAROL: Because Sunday is Easter and I thought we'd go to the sunrise service.

ALICE: Sunrise! You've gotta be kidding!

PETE: Yeah, Alice will hafta get up at three in the morning in order to get her hair and face ready for the world to see her!

ALICE: Well, the world'll never be ready to see your face!

BILL: I wonder if other families go through all of this. I mean, I see all these other people coming to worship with smiles on their faces — they look happy and excited to be there. Why can't we be like that?

CAROL: I'm not sure we're so unique, Bill. That's why we need to hear the message of Easter. We need to know that God loves us and forgives us in spite of our selfishness and self-centeredness. I'm not sure I was always excited about going to worship when I was a kid. But, I'm glad I went. It has helped me grow in my faith. I think these two will grow to appreciate what it means as they mature also.

ALICE: Okay, okay, I'll go. But, how about if we go out to brunch afterwards. I'd like to show off my new Easter dress.

BILL: What new Easter dress?

ALICE: The one we're going shopping for tonight, right, Mom?

CAROL: We had talked about it.

BILL: Okay, a new dress and brunch it is. But, let's not have any more complaining about going to worship. I think we should be glad we can go. Some people don't have that privilege. We do and we should take advantage of it.

CAROL: Holy week and Easter really is a special time. It reminds us of how great God's love is for us and it enables us to celebrate our salvation.

PETE: I'm gonna go call my friends about coming over on Friday night. They will like that service with the lights going off — it's cool. *(Exits)*

ALICE: And I'm going to finish my homework. I should be ready to go shopping right after dinner, Mom. *(Exits)*

BILL: Well, at least we got that settled.

CAROL: And I think they will be okay about going to worship. Those special services have a way of speaking to a person and reminding us of what Christ really did for us.

BILL: I hope you're right. It's certainly a message we all need to hear. Well, if you are going shopping right after dinner, I suppose we'd better get started on making it.

(Both start walking out)

CAROL: Good idea. What are you planning to make?

— The End —

www.ingramcontent.com/pod-product-compliance
Lightning Source LLC
Chambersburg PA
CBHW060853050426
42453CB00008B/967